March 2013

P9-BAU-804

Rookie
Read-About®
Dinosaurs

Apatosaurus

by Wil Mara

Content Consultant

Gregory M. Erickson, PhD
Paleontologist
The Florida State University
Tallahassee, Florida

Reading Consultant

Jeanne Clidas
Reading Specialist

DISCARDED

Children's Press®
An Imprint of Scholastic Inc.
New York Toronto London Auckland Sydney
Mexico City New Delhi Hong Kong
Danbury, Connecticut

Library of Congress Cataloging-in-Publication Data
Mara, Wil.
  Apatosaurus / by Wil Mara.
    p. cm. — (Rookie read-about dinosaurs)
  Includes bibliographical references and index.
  ISBN-13: 978-0-531-20865-6 (lib. bdg.)   ISBN-10: 0-531-20865-6 (lib. bdg.)
  ISBN-13: 978-0-531-20934-9 (pbk.)   ISBN-10: 0-531-20934-2 (pbk.)
  1. Apatosaurus—Juvenile literature. I. Title.
  QE862.S3M3334 2012
  567.913'8—dc23   2011033328

© 2012 by Scholastic Inc. All rights reserved.
Printed in China 62

SCHOLASTIC, CHILDREN'S PRESS, ROOKIE READ-ABOUT®, and associated
logos are trademarks and/or registered trademarks of Scholastic Inc.

1 2 3 4 5 6 7 8 9 10 R 21 20 19 18 17 16 15 14 13 12

Photographs © 2012: Bridgeman Art Library/Look and Learn: 10; Courtesy
of Dinosaur Resource Center, Woodland Park, Colorado: 28, 29; Everett
Collection/Mary Evans Picture Library : 8, 31 top left; Getty Images: 14, 15,
31 top right (De Agostini Picture Library), 24 (Dorling Kindersley), 20, 21, 31
bottom right (Field Museum Library), 6 (Sam Panthaky/AFP); iStockphoto/
JoeLena: 16, 17; Photo Researchers/Richard Bizley: 18; Superstock, Inc.: 26
(De Agostini), 4, 31 bottom left (dieKleinert), cover (NHPA); The Image Works/
The Natural History Museum: 22, 23.

TABLE OF CONTENTS

MEET THE APATOSAURUS

The Apatosaurus (uh-pah-tuh-SAWR-uss) was a huge dinosaur. It ate plants. It did not eat meat.

The babies hatched from eggs. The eggs were very big.

8

The Apatosaurus lived a long life. Some lived to be 100 years old.

HOW BIG WAS BIG?

The Apatosaurus was one of the biggest animals ever.

The Apatosaurus was longer than two school buses.
It weighed as much as four elephants.

Its legs were thick.

They were as thick as tree trunks.

HOW DID THE APATOSAURUS EAT?

The Apatosaurus had a long neck. It used its neck to reach plants on the ground.

The Apatosaurus ate trees.
It used its neck to reach
leaves up high.

GETTING AROUND

The Apatosaurus moved
very slowly.

The Apatosaurus had a very long tail.

It helped this dinosaur keep its balance.

FIGHTING

The Apatosaurus had a big,
sharp claw on each foot.
It used its claws to fight
its enemies.

The Apatosaurus could chase away other animals with its tail.

DINOSAUR BONES

Scientists found
Apatosaurus bones. They
built a skeleton from the
bones. It is in a museum.

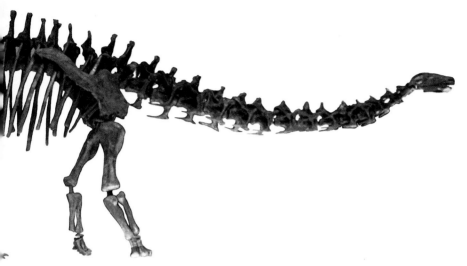

Can you find the long tail and long neck bones on this skeleton? Can you find the huge leg bones?

TRY THIS! Help your child understand the size comparisons in this book by going back to page 12. You can point out that the long neck and tail on the skeleton helped scientists to know the Apatosaurus was as long as two school buses. The thick leg bones helped scientists to estimate this dinosaur's weight.

APATOSAURUS FACT FILE

The name Apatosaurus means "deceptive lizard."

Apatosaurus eggs were the size of soccer balls.

Visit this Scholastic web site for more information on the Apatosaurus:
www.factsfornow.scholastic.com

WORDS YOU KNOW

Apatosaurus

leg

neck

tail

Index

Learn More!

You can learn more about the Apatosaurus at:

www.amnh.org/exhibitions/permanent/fossilhalls/vertebrate/specimens/apatosaurus.php

About the Author

Wil Mara is the award-winning author of more than 100 books, many of them educational titles for young readers. More information about his work can be found at *www.wilmara.com*.